T0115745

THE HAUNTED TEA-COSY

A Dispirited and Distasteful Diversion for Christmas

EDWARD GOREY

DEY ST.
AN IMPRINT OF
WILLIAM MORROW PUBLISHERS

Copyright © 1997 by Edward Gorey

All rights reserved. No part of this publication may be
reproduced or transmitted in any form or by any means,
electronic or mechanical, including photocopy, recording,
or any information storage and retrieval system,
without permission in writing from the publisher.

No part of this book may be used or reproduced in any manner whatsoever without written permission except in the case of brief quotations embodied in critical articles and reviews.

For information, address HarperCollins Publishers, 195 Broadway, New York, NY 10007.

The Haunted Tea-Cosy first appeared in the December 21, 1997
issue of *The New York Times Magazine*.

ISBN: 0-15-100415-3

Printed in Vietnam

23 RRDA 15 14 13 12 11 10 9

To the memory of Matthew Green

Edmund Gravel, known as the Recluse of Lower Spigot to everybody there and elsewhere, prepared to take tea by himself on Christmas Eve.

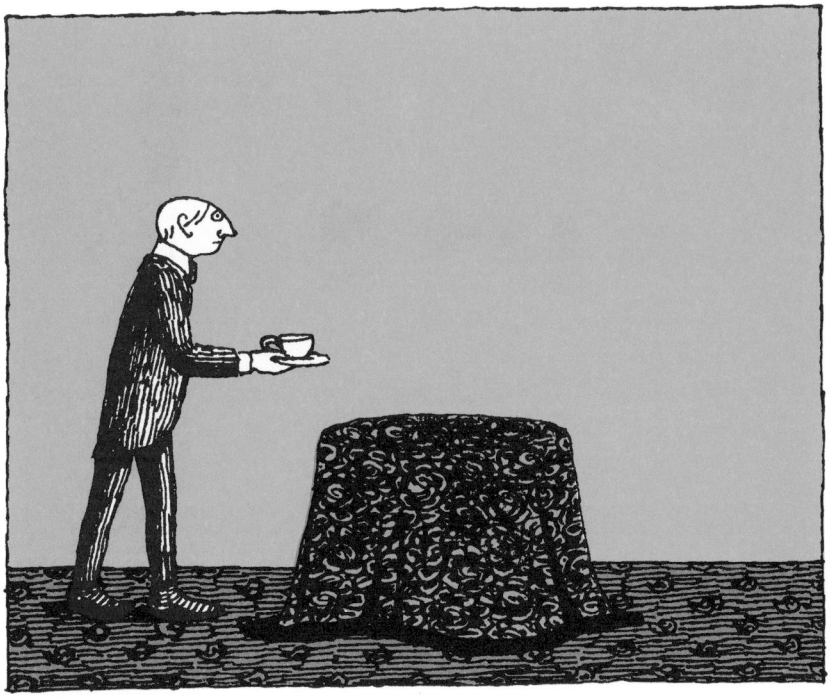

He was hardly able to cut a slice of fruitcake from the last one he had received more than a decade ago.

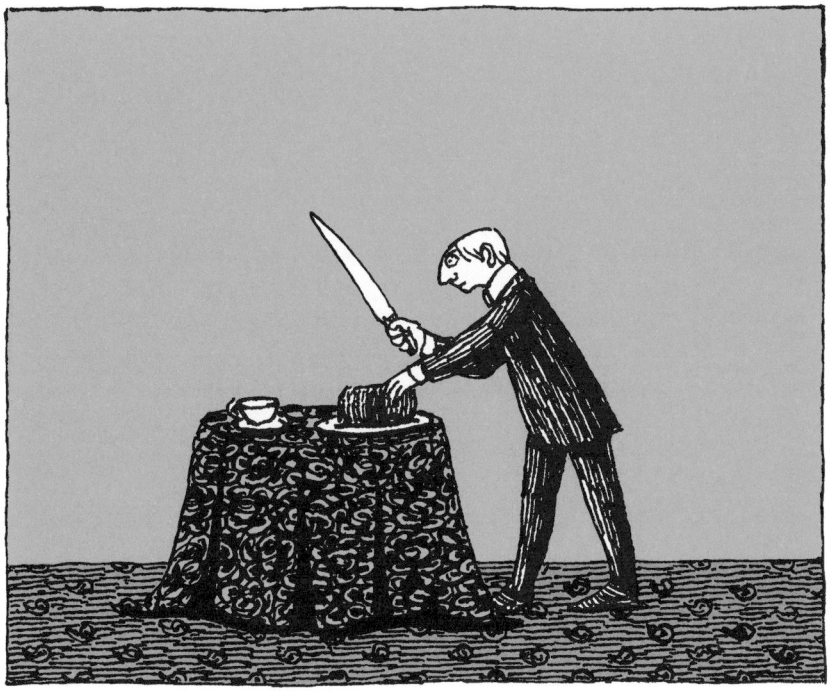

Waiting for the week's teabag to steep,
he wrote by hand several letters to
the newspapers anent the price of
a typewriter ribbon having risen
the day of the winter solstice.

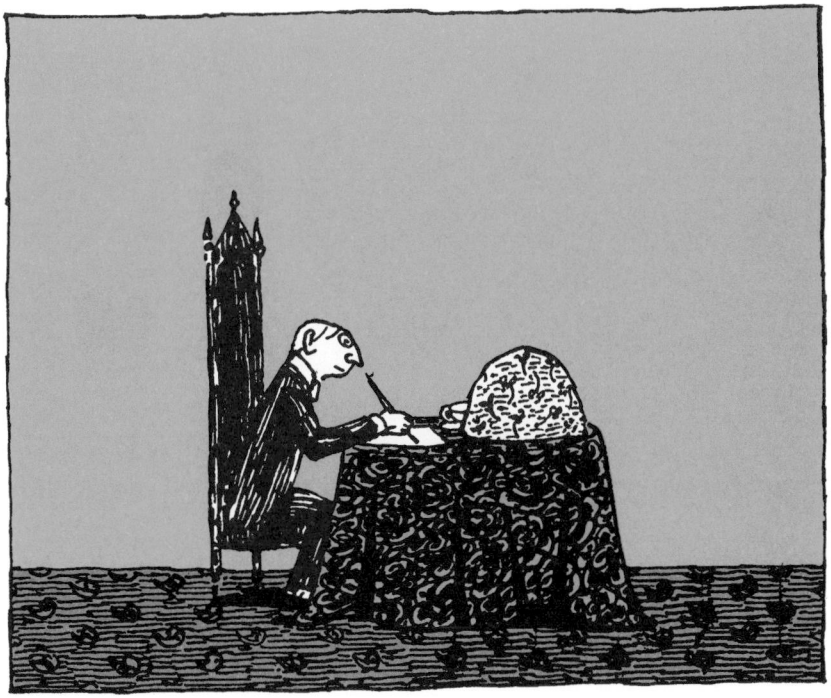

The tea-cosy suddenly twitched and from beneath it leapt a creature many times the size of the space within, even if it had not already held the teapot.

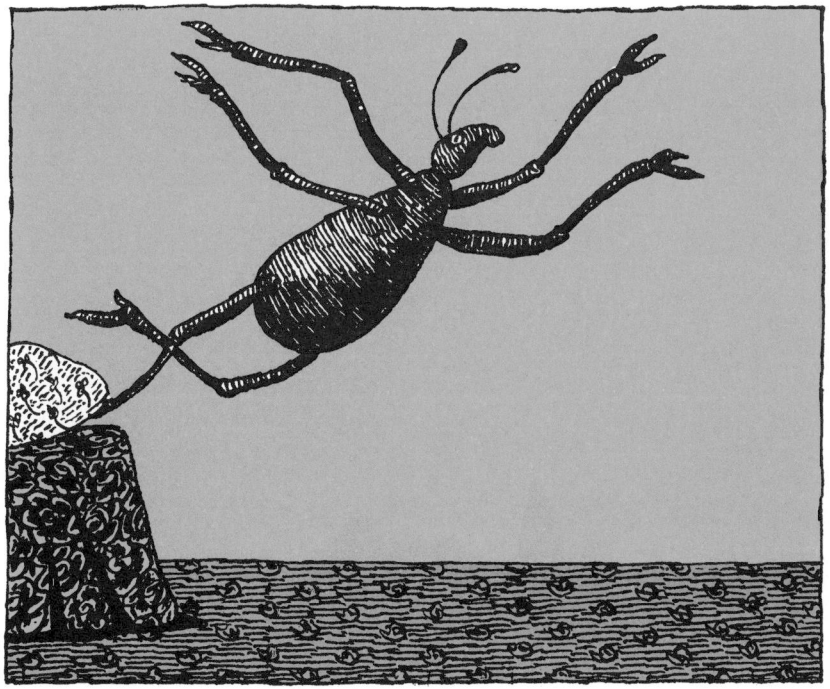

'I am the Bahhum Bug,' it declared;
'I am here to diffuse the interests
of didacticism.'

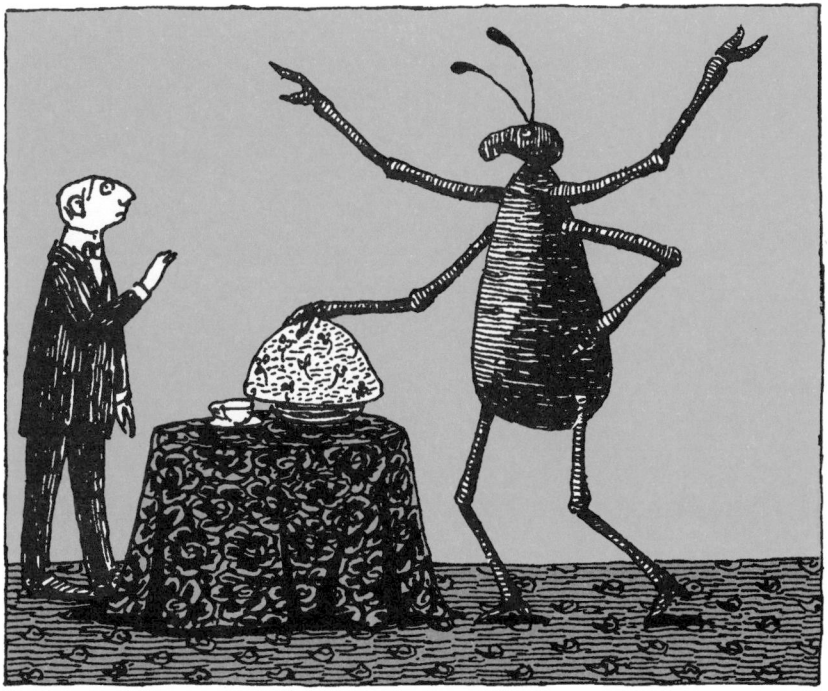

A knocking was heard at the door through which, without it opening, stepped a subfuse but transparent personage.

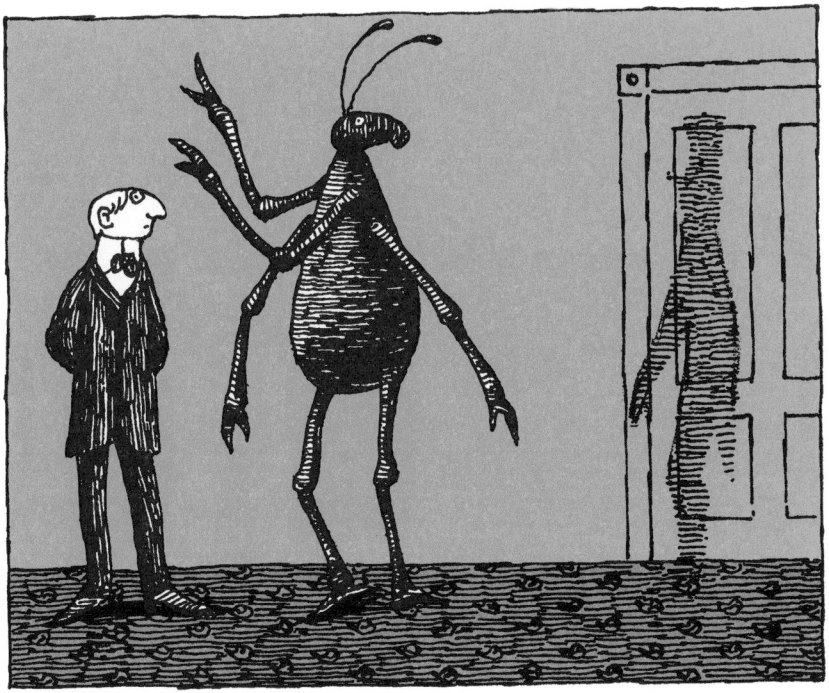

'I am the Spectre of Christmas That Never Was,' it muttered, 'and I have come to show you Affecting Scenes.'

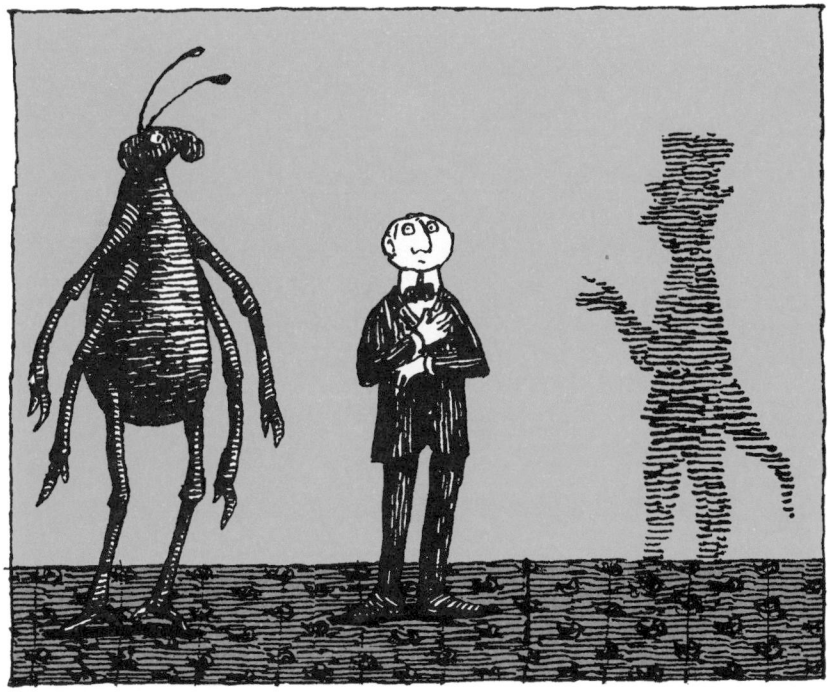

Gravel and his companions found themselves at a great distance somewhere to the north.

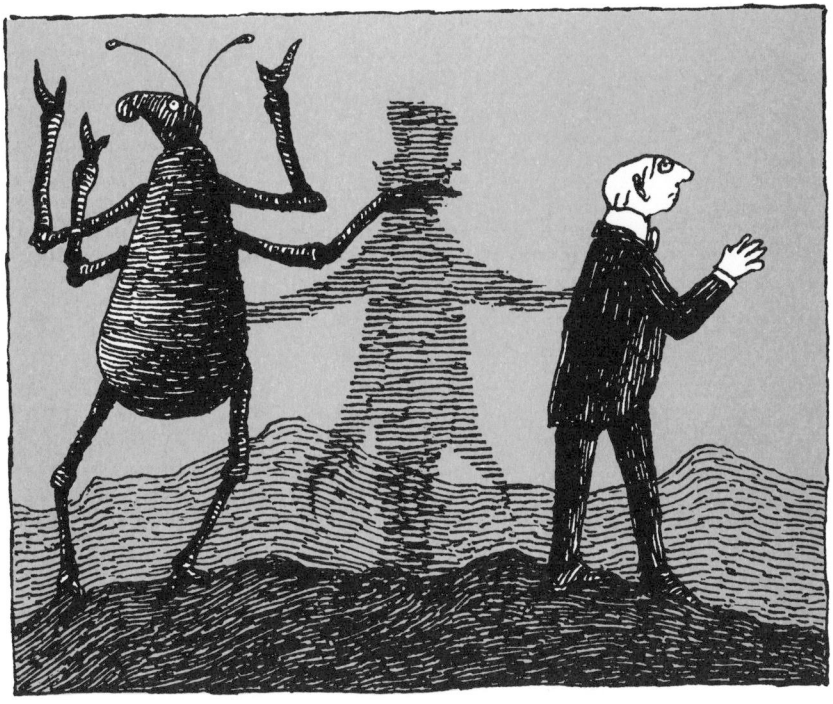

A small orphan called Nub and a
large stray dog named Bruno
huddled against a tombstone
whose inscription was worn away.

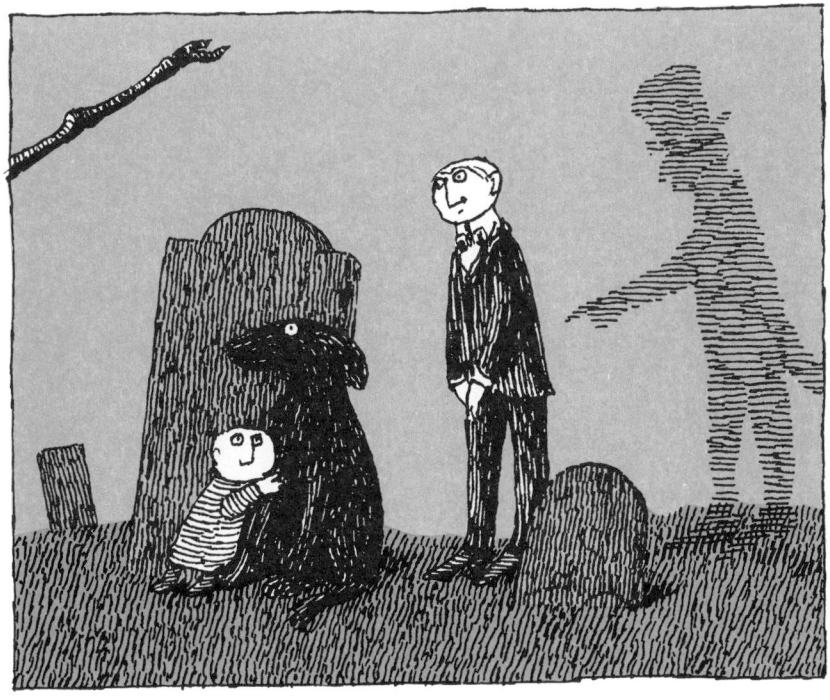

Across the road from the churchyard Alberta Stipple returned home to find the wallpaper in the drawing room gone.

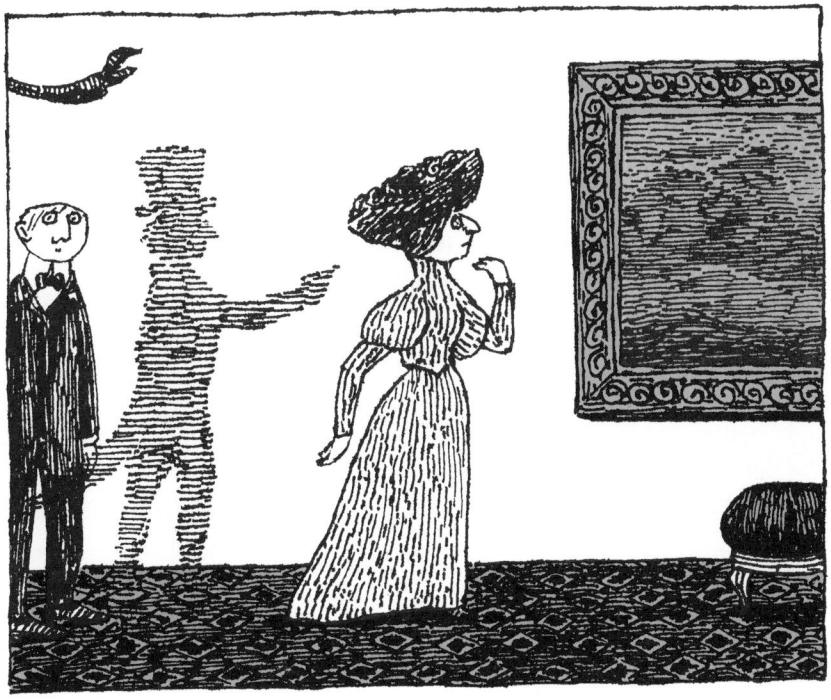

Three doors to the east the Edward Boggles could not agree whether the grandfather clock was fast or slow.

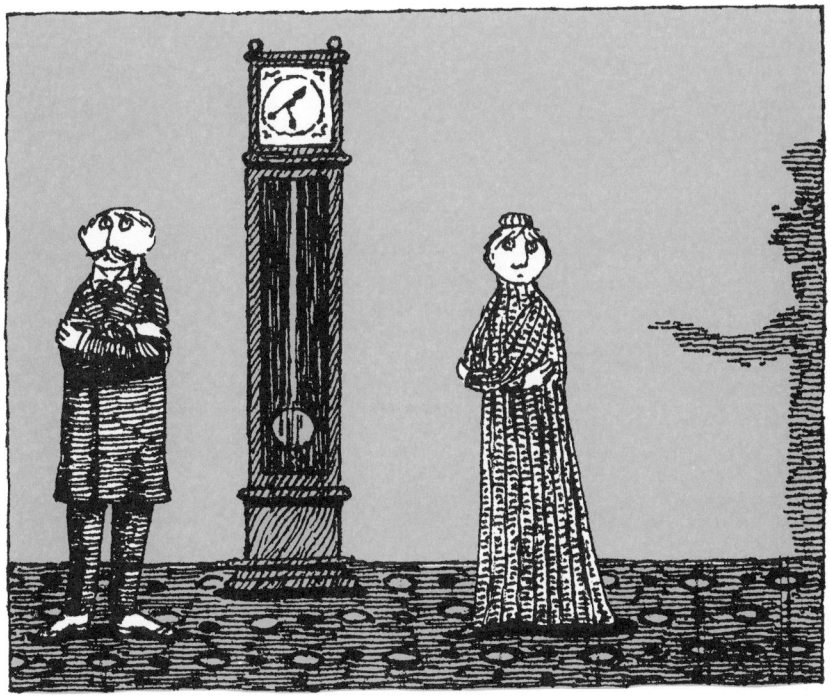

In the high street of the village
Reverend Flannel lost his tuning-
fork.

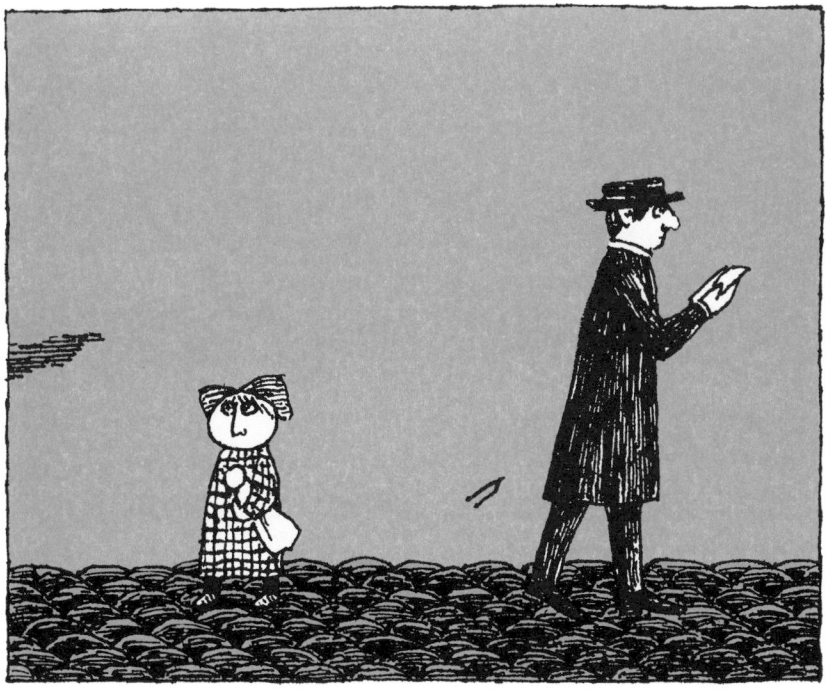

In the cottage next to the post office Alma Crumble broke her wrist stirring batter, at which the Bug declared in a minatory tone that 'That was enough of that.'

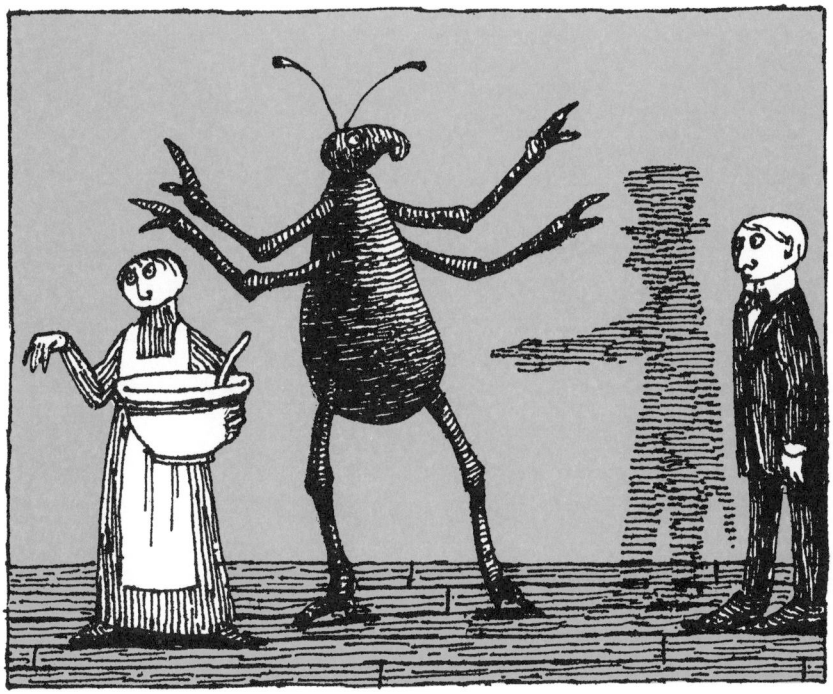

No sooner were they back than a twittering was heard outside the window through which, without breaking the glass, drifted a second subfusc but transparent personage.

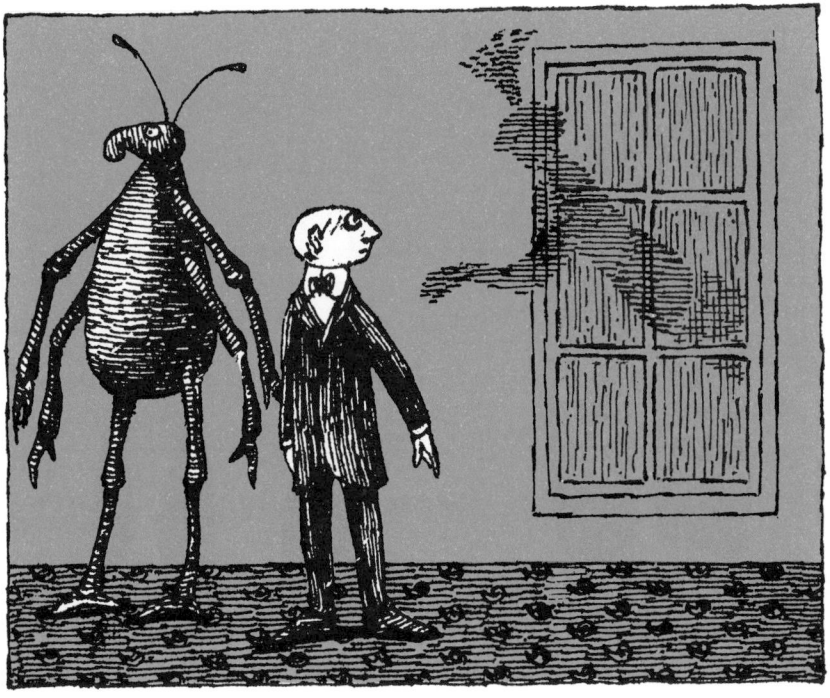

'I am the Spectre of Christmas That Isn't,' it murmured, 'and I have come to show you Distressing Scenes.'

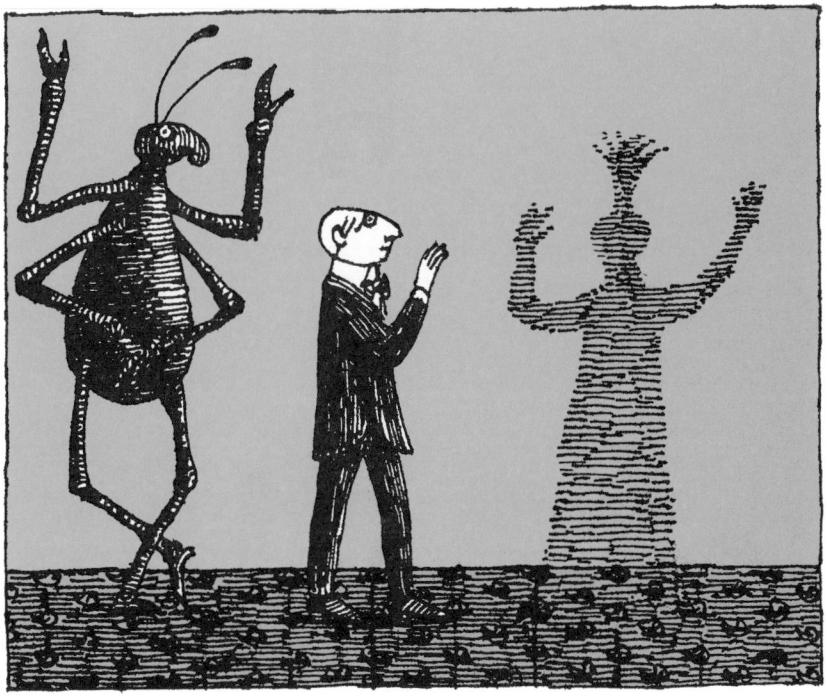

Albinia Fennel reclined on a chaise longue and waited for a letter from her brother in far-off Hokkaido, Japan.

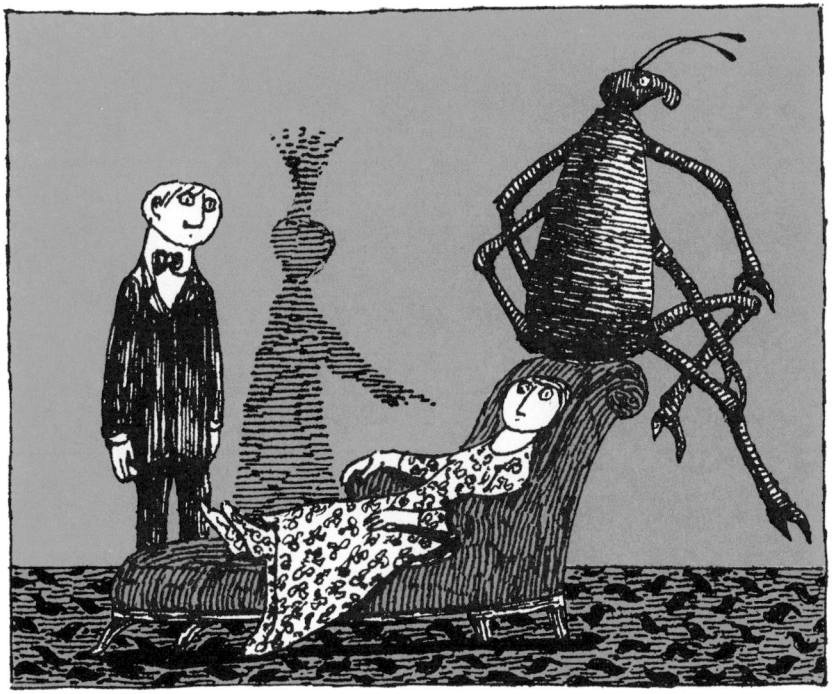

Over the way Alfreda Scumble was abstracted from the veranda by gypsies despite the barks of Nero.

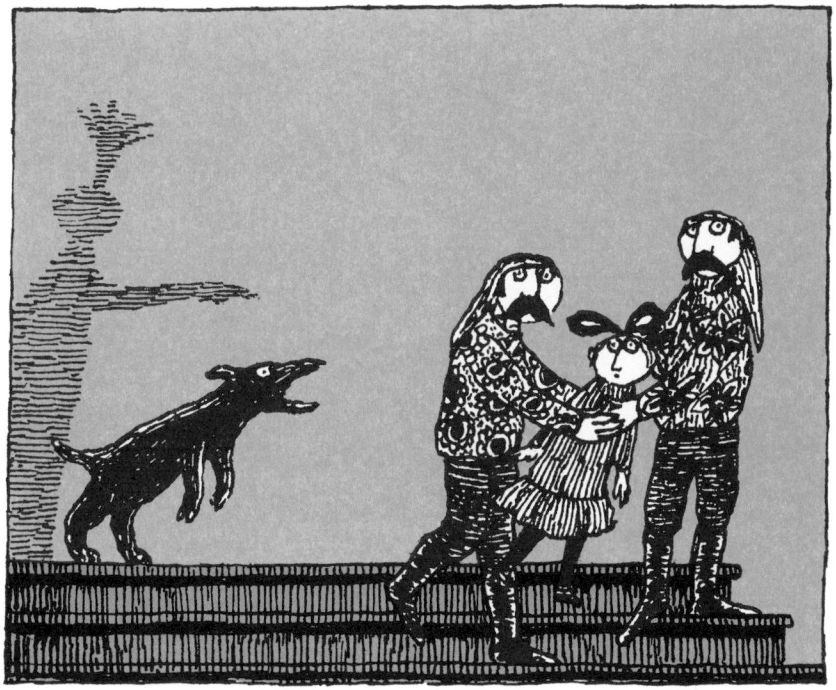

Next door but one the Edgar Grapples,
Senior and Junior, had an argument
as to what day of the week it was.

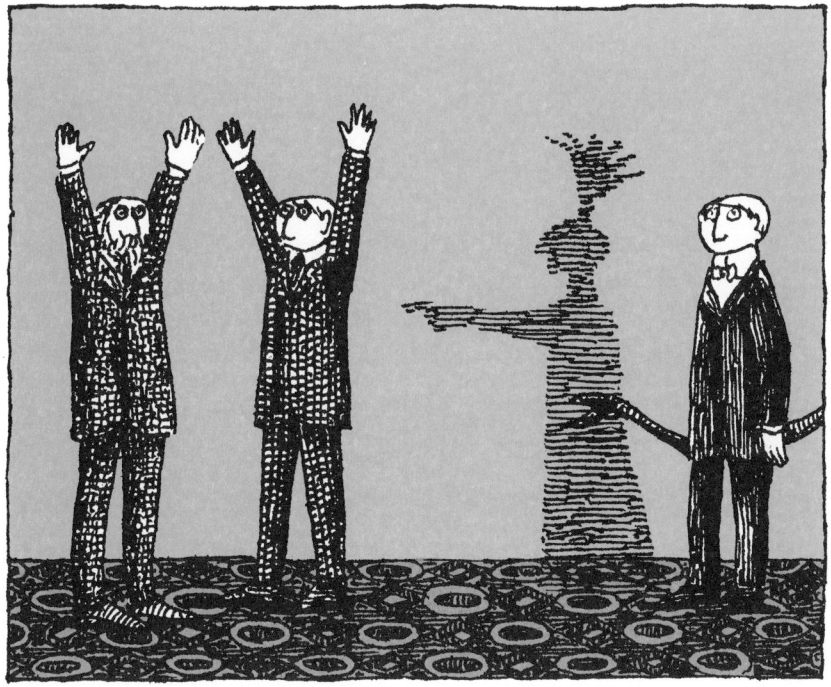

To the south, in the cemetery a wrong coffin in a newly dug grave was found to contain rolls of used wallpaper.

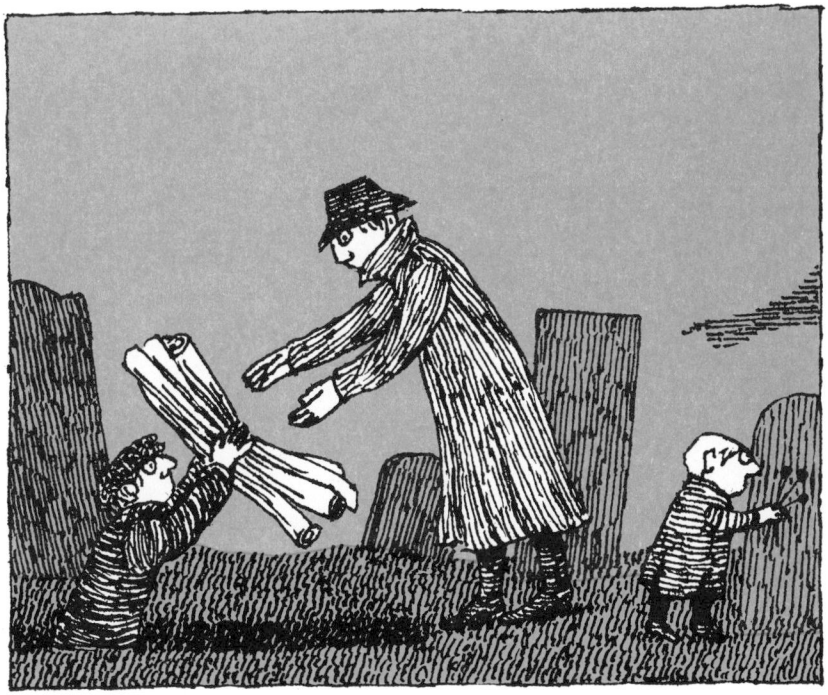

In a nearby villa Edo Haggle sprained his ankle while playing billiards, at which the Bug declared in an admonitory tone that 'That is enough of that.'

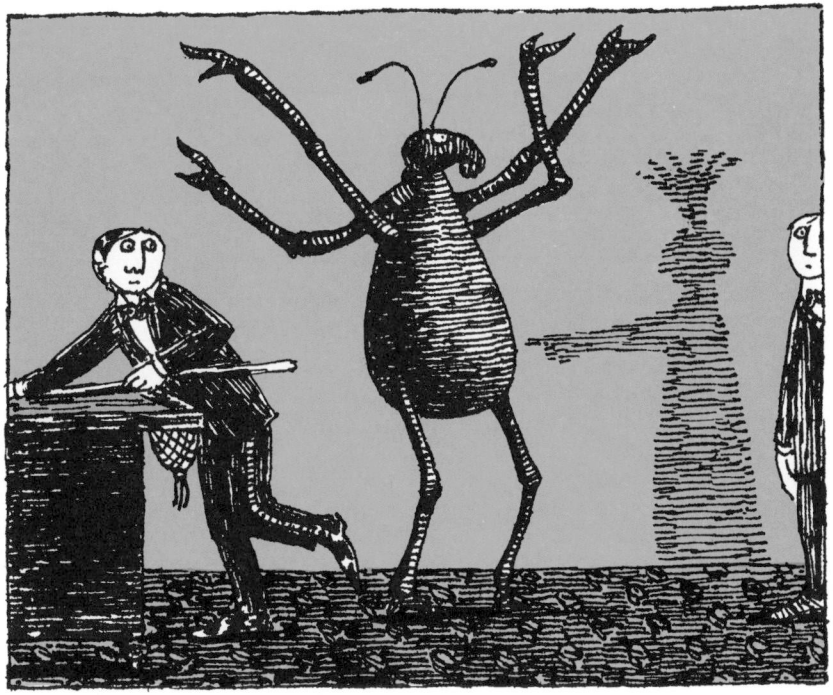

No sooner were they back than a scratching came from under the floor through which, without disturbing the boards, ascended a third subfusc but transparent personage.

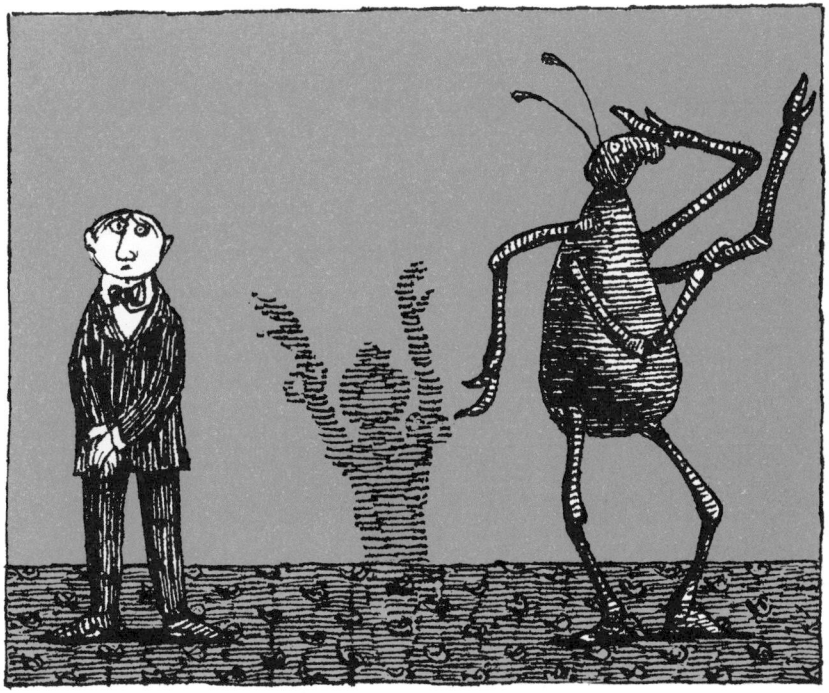

'I am the Spectre of Christmas That Never Will Be,' it mumbled, 'and I have come to show you Heart-Rending Scenes.'

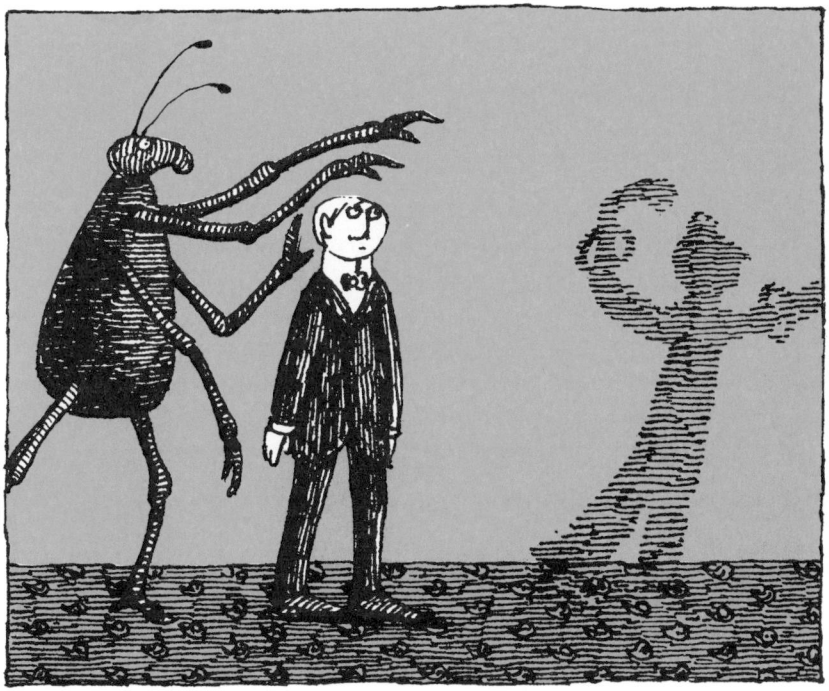

Alicia Grumble woke in the night unable to think where she had put her Bible.

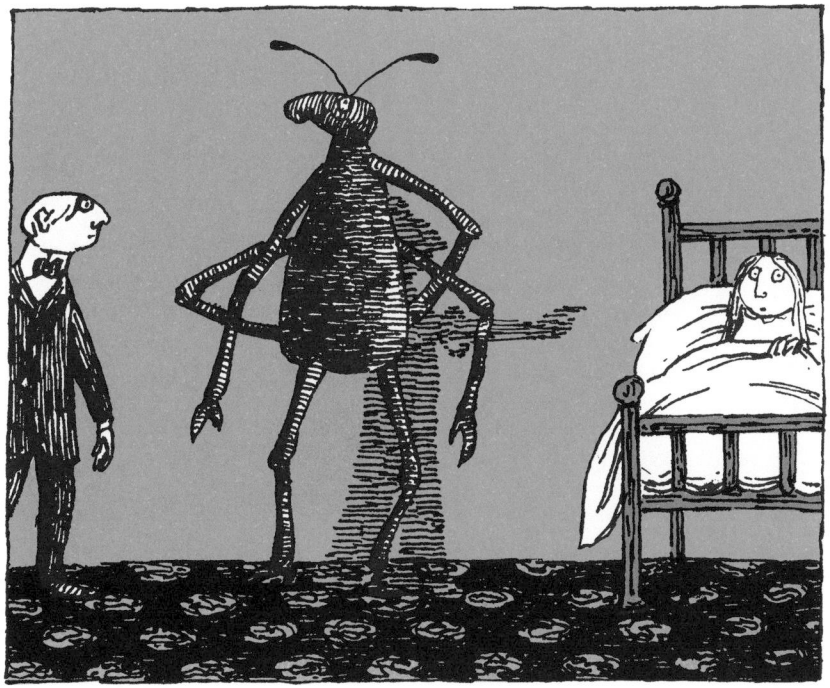

To the house opposite Fido was returned
from the taxidermist and set down
by the fireplace.

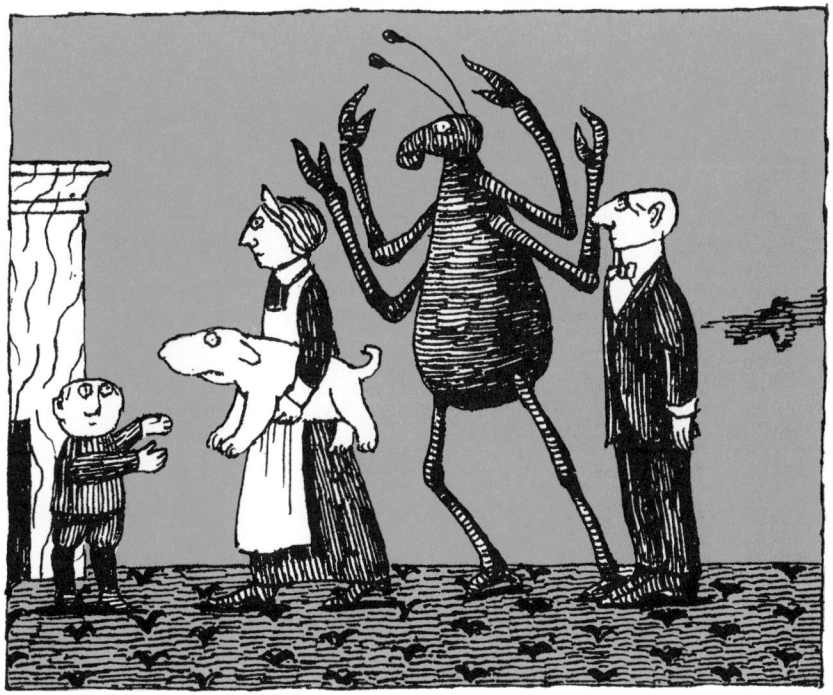

In a residence to the west Alethea Funnel lay on the sofa remembering her fiancé who had gone down with the Alexandra.

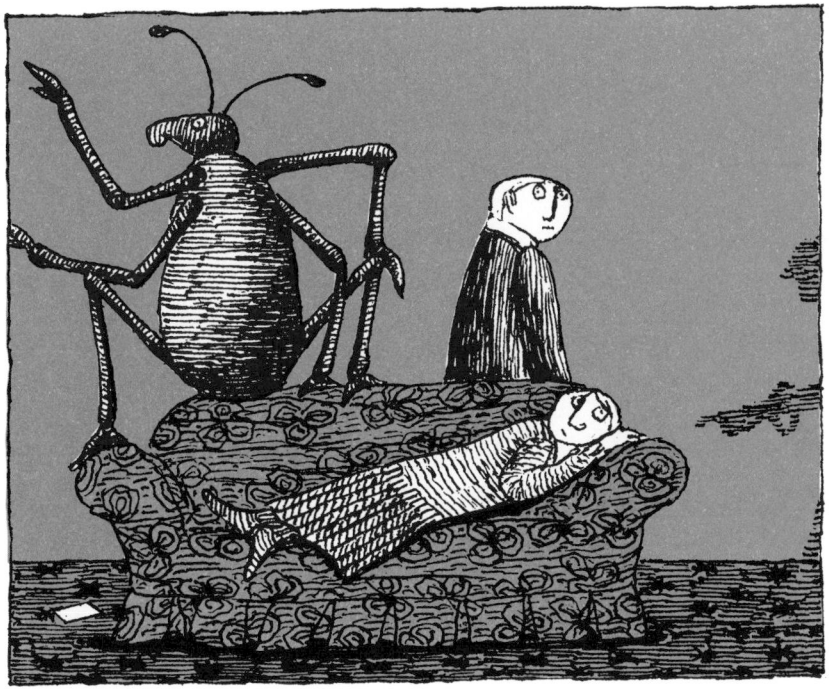

Beyond, at the ancestral home Lady Snaggle was informed her husband's were the brains behind an international gang of wallpaper thieves.

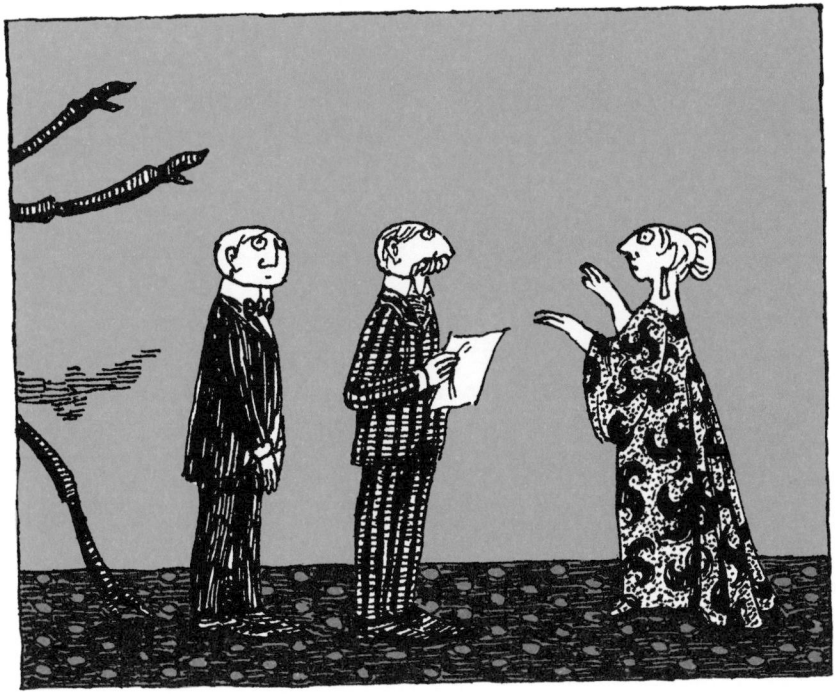

At the lodge Edwin Stopple, attempting to deal with a loose slate, fell off the roof, at which the Bug declared in an objurgatory tone that 'That will be enough of that.'

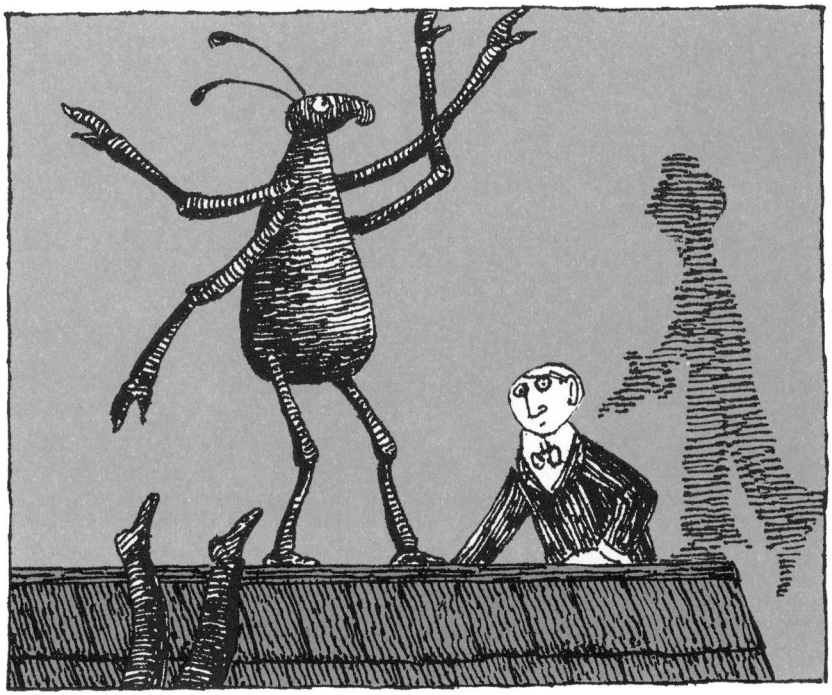

No sooner were they back than Gravel cried, 'I shall give a party and ask everyone in Lower Spigot and others from elsewhere,' and plunged into penning invitations.

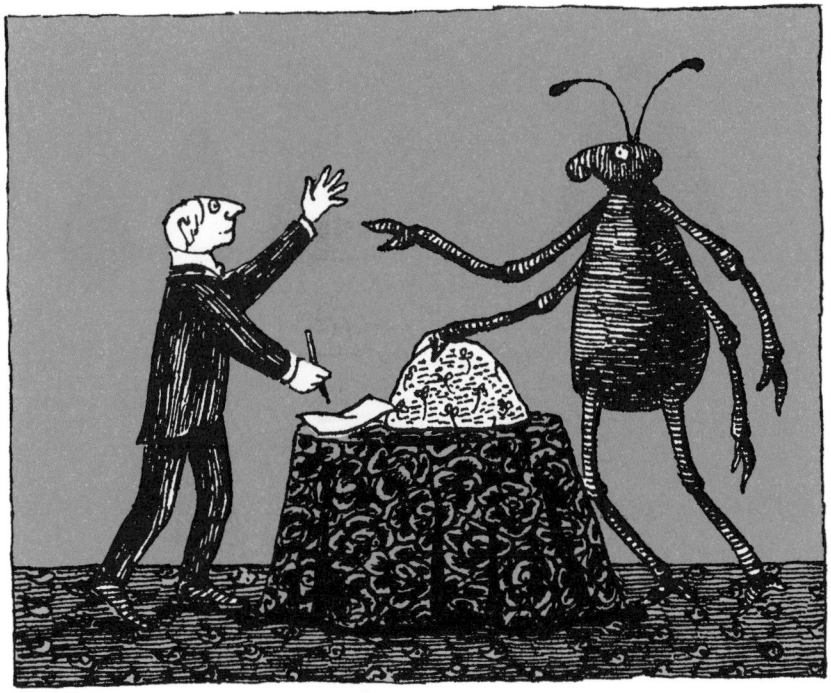

The cynosure was a cake taller
than anything else in the room,
a conflation of Chartres Cathedral
and the Stupa at Borobudur iced
in dazzling white sugar; inside
was a quarter-ton of fruitcake.

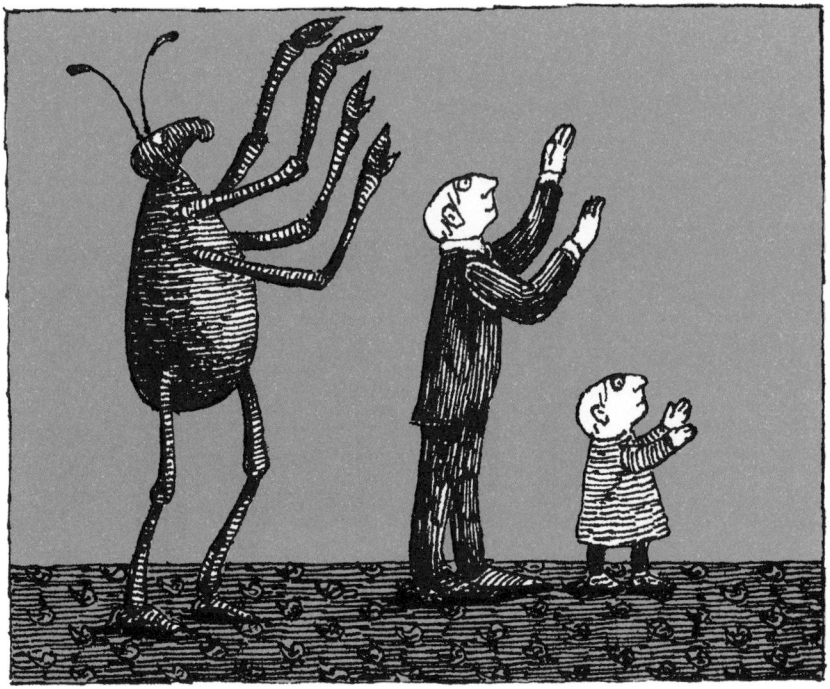

Giggling, dancing, and shrieking prevailed and, as the evening wore on, were carried to the very edge of the unseemly.

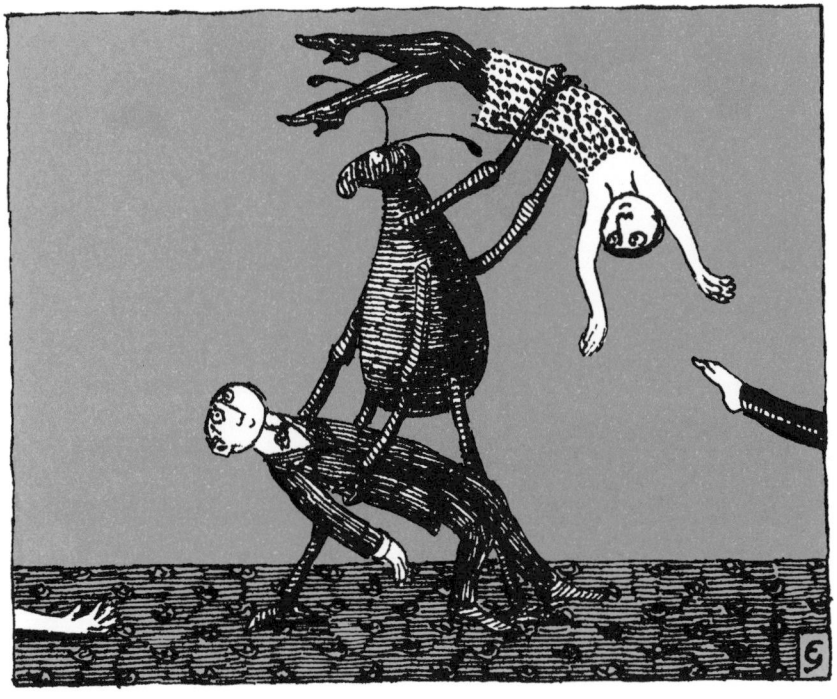